501 EXCUSES to Play Golf

Justin J. Exner

SOURCEBOOKS HYSTERIA™
AN IMPRINT OF SOURCEBOOKS, INC.®
NAPERVILLE, ILLINOIS

Published by Sourcebooks, Inc.
P.O. Box 4410, Naperville, Illinois 60567-4410
(630) 961-3900
FAX: (630) 961-2168
www.sourcebooks.com

Originally published in 2000

Library of Congress Cataloging-in-Publication Data

Exner, Justin J.
  501 excuses to play golf / by Justin J. Exner.
     p. cm.
  ISBN 1-4022-0255-5 (alk. paper)
  1. Golf—Humor. I. Title: Five hundred one excuses to play golf. II. Title.
GV967 .E98 2004
796.352'02—dc22

                                        2003023433

Printed and bound in the United States of America
VP   10   9   8   7   6   5   4   3   2

I am thankful for the many blessings in my life,
including my wonderful wife, Dawn.

I also dedicate this to my children.
Never let anyone convince you that you are not good enough.
You can accomplish whatever you choose to do.

You should never need an excuse to play golf but...

Since I had to drive all the way to another city to help you move, I'm sure going to golf.

The doctor said that after getting an injection, I should keep my arms loose. Golfing is the best thing.

With the economy the way it is, I need to take up a new sport.

The weather has been so bad lately—I want to take advantage of the sunny weather.

-5-
I finished all my projects at work.

-6-
Since winning the lottery,
I need something to occupy my time.

-7-
My father's will said I had to
spend the money on greens fees!

-8-
I need practice; the Masters
is on TV next week.

2

−9−

I was motivated to qualify for
the U.S. Open.

−10−

I have to get used to my new putter.

−11−

I received a new sleeve of
balls for my birthday.

−12−

My wife is due with our first child.
I have to play as much as
possible before he's born.

-13-

I really need some form of exercise.

-14-

I have been working way too hard;
I need to relax.

-15-

The storm knocked out the electricity,
so the office is closed.

-16-

The IT department won't be able to
fix the server till next Monday,
so we are taking the week off.

4

-17-

I need quality time with my friends.

-18-

The doctor recommended I golf every day...
or at least I think that's what he said!

-19-

I'm eager to find out if my visualization
exercises actually work under pressure.

-20-

It's the only thing I can do at 5:30 A.M.

5

-21-

The courses are too busy on the weekends,
so I'm going out today.

-22-

The lawn mower is broken.

-23-

My wife went to a baby shower
and I have nothing to do.

-24-

I've set a goal for myself:
play 54 holes in one day.

–25–

The wind may help
me reach the
par–5s in two.

7

-26-
Someone asked.

-27-
It's Father's Day; I'll do what I want.

-28-
It's a requirement at the next sales meeting.

-29-
I need to work on my tan.
It's never cloudy on a golf course.

-30-

I got a gift certificate for a free round of golf for my birthday.

-31-

Greens fees are half-price before noon.

-32-

The British Open has me all excited.

-33-

I am almost 50; I need to practice for the Senior Tour.

9

-34-

I like to see the beautiful
swans on the pond.

-35-

It's the perfect place to get together
and discuss life with coworkers.

-36-

My email is down at the office.

-37-

It is rumored they lowered the
cost of beer at the course.

-38-
I heard a new tee box was added.

-39-
I've been invited to play on the best-kept course in town.

-40-
I have two teenage daughters—
I need something to take my mind
off what they're up to.

-41-
My car broke down right
in front of the golf course.

-42-

My son was suspended from school.
I thought I'd take him golfing so
we could have a heart-to-heart talk.

-43-

My brother-in-law has a layover
on his way east, so I thought we
could catch up while playing nine.

-44-

I can expense it for business purposes.

-45-

I have a few hours to kill before
the M*A*S*H reruns start.

12

-46-

I wasn't able to golf in the outing
last week, so I'll go today.

-47-

I collect used tees in all the tee boxes.

-48-

I need to work on my game,
and I'm not really in the mood
to go to the range.

-49-

I always meet interesting
people on the course.

-50-

The golf course is the only place I get good customer service.

-51-

The grass is too wet to cut, so
I might just as well go golfing.

-52-

It was such a long winter;
this spring weather makes me feel like golfing.

-53-

I need to teach my son how to drive.
The golf cart is the perfect instructional tool.

-54-

My old neighbor invited me to golf on a
course I haven't played since I moved away.

15

-55-

I was furloughed from the Union job,
so I have plenty of free time.

-56-

My girlfriend asked me to go
away for a few hours.

-57-

My wife took lessons, so now
I have to take her out on the course.

-58-

I got a super deal on a golf package.

-59-
There are excellent fairway
bunkers on this course.

-60-
I have to teach my son-in-law how to play.

-61-
There is an opportunity to
see a celebrity on the course.

-62-
I have been practicing putting on my carpet;
now I want to see if the
practice has paid off.

17

-63-

I have never had the chance to
play golf in Arizona.

-64-

They say the greens are tough in Myrtle.
I have to try it for myself.

-65-

My wife wants to have sex—I'm going golfing.

-66-

The course is allowing me to
demo clubs for free today.

18

-67-

I got my new handicap card and
want to show the guys at the club.

-68-

We're on vacation, and my family
wants me to be happy.

-69-

I have never had an eagle
before and I feel lucky.

-70-

The clubs are the only things
I've got until the movers arrive.

-71-

It's the first day above 50 degrees.

-72-

They are offering 18 holes for the price of 9.

-73-

The fish aren't biting this time of year.

-74-

The bowling alley was closed.

20

-76-

The Cubs missed the wild card,
so my afternoons are free.

-77-

I could finally afford a pair of name brand
clubs—I want to see if I can break 120!

-78-

I got a new beer coolie.
I have to try it out on the course.

-79-

I had the pin shot at league play
and won free greens fees.

-80-
I had back surgery recently.
I need to see if it helped!

-81-
I went to the ballet last night, so my
wife is letting me go golfing today.

-82-
It's the only place I know where
I can get a free pencil.

-83-
I have to try my new sand wedge.

-84-

I need to get some lawn care tips from the ground maintenance crew.

-85-

They have a great microbrewery at the clubhouse.

-86-

They opened a nursery in the clubhouse, and I want to find out how good their baby-sitter is.

-87-

I heard they have been double-cutting the greens. I just have to try them out.

-88-

I have to try out my new golf visor.

-89-

I got a new pair of knickers.

-90-

Last time I was out, I had a hole in one.
I want to see if I can do it again.

-91-

They have really soft toilet paper
at the golf course.

25

-92-

The course serves a great
club sandwich for lunch.

-93-

My wife told me to go golfing;
she was having the girls over.

-94-

It's not raining as hard as it was yesterday.

-95-

I heard demo clubs are being offered
with every green fee paid!

-96-

The interior of my house is being painted.
I need to get out for a couple of hours.

-97-

My car is being fixed...again!

-98-

My kids are all away at camp.

-99-

My wife was yelling at me, so
I decided to get out of the house.

–100–

I have to see if these new golf balls are really easier to see in a cloudy sky.

28

-101-

It's a three-day weekend and my wife has to work—I'm not going to do chores.

-102-

I enjoy looking for my ball in the rough.

-103-

It's the only fun thing I can do with my family.

-104-

I'm locked out of the house. I only have the keys to the car trunk where my clubs are.

-105-

I have new glasses; I have to see
if I can follow the ball.

-106-

My girlfriend went to the movies,
and I need to kill a few hours.

-107-

It's the first day of spring;
I might as well go golfing.

-108-

I have to test my new allergy medicine.

-109-

The movers are packing my house.
I have nothing else to do.

-110-

I missed the shuttle bus to go to work.

-111-

The golf course serves the best
canned beer in the city.

-112-

I'm trying to conserve energy, and
the course uses electric carts.

-113-
I got lost going to work and
ended up at the golf course.

-114-
I was the one-millionth shopper and
I was given a year's worth of greens fees.

-115-
My doctor instructed me to
take up a non-stressful sport!

-116-
I have to see if I eliminated my slice.

-117-

I've been practicing at the range every day.
I need to see how I'll do on the real course.

-118-

My dad always pays when we go.

-119-

I work nights; I have nothing
else to do during the day.

-120-

I'm home shopping, and the realtor is
taking me golfing to show me a few houses.

33

-121-

I have to get out as much as possible.
Here in Alaska we can only play
golf four months a year.

-122-

I'm out of beer at home, so I thought
I'd just get some while I golf.

-123-

The rough is really playable on this course.

-124-

My dog ran away and he
always goes to the golf course.
Good dog!

-126-

My tires are being changed.
I need to kill a couple of hours.

-127-

It's an absolutely beautiful day out;
I can't possibly go to work.

-128-

I haven't played since last summer.

-129-

I heard the traps at this
course were really tough.

–130–
It's league play day.

–131–
Summer is almost over, and
I just have not played enough.

–132–
My wife is making me go!

–133–
I need to break in my new golf shoes.

-134-

Winter is coming and I need
to get out as much as possible.

-135-

I need to try out my new
double titanium krypton driver with
atomic shaft and sand grooved grips.

-136-

Tomorrow is ladies' day,
so I have to get out today.

-137-

My golf pro said I had
to get out much more often.

38

-138-

I am sick of playing golf on my computer.
I want to play for real.

-139-

I got those new golf balls that fly "too far,"
and I have to try them out.

-140-

The driving range is closed for repairs;
I have to practice somewhere.

-141-

I just got an 87-degree wedge that if
swung properly, will send the ball backwards.

39

-142-
Senior citizens get a discount this year!

-143-
I sprayed my balls with silicon spray, which guarantees my ball won't slice.

-144-
I bought those new golf contact lenses, guaranteed to cut 5 strokes off your score.

-145-
My doctor told me to walk as much as possible. I might as well walk from the cart to my ball!

-146-

They put new tee boxes on the par—5s.

-147-

The weather forecast next month is for rain;
I need to get in as much golf as possible.

-148-

I'm in love with the beer—cart girl.
I think this is the real thing.

-149-

I read somewhere that golfing is
good for the back.

41

–151–

I am required to golf for work;
I love my job.

–152–

The phone lines are down at work.

–153–

I have been taking vitamins,
which are supposed to allow me to
hit the ball an extra ten yards.

–154–

Why not go golfing?

43

-155-
I need to get out on the course
before it snows any more.

-156-
They didn't promote me at work,
so I am taking as much time off as possible.

-157-
My game is starting to come together,
and I need to keep sharp.

-158-
My kid wanted to see if he could beat me.

44

–159–

I lost all the skins last week;
I need to try and win the money back.

–160–

My boss needed a fourth.

–161–

My son is sick and he asked
me to fill in for him.

–162–

The course just opened.

45

-163-

Last week I almost broke 100.
I have to keep trying.

-164-

I just had laser eye surgery.
I want to see if it helps me
follow the ball in flight.

-165-

What else would I do on vacation?

-166-

I like taking the perfect divot.

-167-

It's raining, and I need to see if
my new rain gear is effective.

-168-

I have to pay the country club dues;
I might as well get my money's worth.

-169-

My wife said if I cleaned out the garage,
I could go golfing...so I took my clubs
out of the garage and here I am.

-170-

The weather is beautiful.

47

-171-

I have to keep trying to get the hole in one.

-172-

I have a rain check from yesterday.

-173-

I have to practice for the
tournament next week.

-174-

A sand trap has been added
to the practice area.

48

-175-
Because I am retired and I can.

49

–176–

I called in sick at work, but
I feel a little better now.

–177–

The course has a special before 7:00 A.M.

–178–

I love nature.

–179–

I need to play twenty times
to get my handicap established.

-180-

I get more work done on the
course than at the office.

-181-

My flight was canceled,
so I need to kill a few hours.

-182-

My wife took the kids on vacation.

-183-

I got the membership as a Christmas gift.

-184-
I won a new set of clubs;
I no longer have to rent them.

-185-
I want to become a professional golfer,
so I need the practice.

-186-
I need to try my new spikeless shoes.

-187-
I have to take my wife golfing at least once
a year; it was in the prenuptial agreement.

52

-188-

I need to find more golf balls,
and it's the best place to look.

-189-

I watched the pros on TV,
and it looks so easy, I want to try it.

-190-

You get a free cup of coffee
if you play 18 holes.

-191-

There are a lot of cool frogs near the ponds.

-192-
My grandfather taught me to golf and
I want to keep his legacy going.

-193-
The golf course is where I write my books.

-194-
They have the best driving range.

-195-
I golf at the outings, hoping to win the car.

54

–196–

I woke up in the parking lot
of the golf course.

–197–

I enjoy driving the golf carts.

–198–

I bought a whole new golf wardrobe.

–199–

There is nothing like a long, slow walk in the
great outdoors, with no one in front of me.

55

-200-

I read that playing golf was good aerobic exercise.

–201–

My wife bought me new clubs for my birthday.

–202–

I liked playing in the sand as a child; I simply continue to enjoy it as an adult (kind of).

–203–

My friend keeps telling me it's fun.

–204–

I bought a golf cart at a rummage sale.

57

–205–

It gets me out of the house.

–206–

Golf teaches me patience, and I need a lesson.

–207–

I needed to see if my clubs would
fit into the trunk of my new car.

–208–

I enjoy hitting things.

-209-

My buddy is the starter, and he sneaks me on the course for free.

-210-

My wife went furniture shopping.

-211-

That's where we are having the family reunion this year.

-212-

I heard golf is much easier when you're sober, so I have to try it.

59

–213–
Playing golf gives my wife and
I time to talk.

–214–
I'm so late for work,
I might as well not even go in.

–215–
The ATM made a mistake;
now I have some extra money.

–216–
They give out free peanuts at the turn.

-217-
The forecast is for snow; we need
to play as much as possible today.

-218-
I only need eleven more rounds
to establish my handicap.

-219-
It's the first day all week it hasn't rained.

-220-
I just received my unemployment check.

-221-

I finished cutting my grass.

-222-

I just bought a new car; I needed to teach
it the way to the golf course.

-223-

The doctor said running is bad,
but walking with golf clubs is OK.

-224-

I have a meeting at the course,
so I might as well play some golf.

62

-225-

I woke up stiff and creaky; playing golf loosens me up.

63

-226-

I am on a personal mission to find
"the perfect golf hole."

-227-

The pool is closed, so I'm going golfing.

-228-

My wife is making me teach her how to golf.

-229-

My hose is broken so I can't wash the car;
I might as well go golfing.

64

-230-

It's the perfect way to get to know my future father-in-law.

-231-

My job is driving me nuts.

-232-

I need to lose some weight.

-233-

It's my wedding anniversary, so I'm going golfing.

65

-234-

My motorcycle broke down right in front of my favorite course.

-235-

My son turned two yesterday. I need to practice so I can show him how to play.

-236-

I like playing scrambles because I can tee it high and let it fly!

-237-

I got kicked out of G.A. (Golfers Anonymous).

–238–

My college roommate is in town, and
it's the only thing we have in common.

–239–

My company sponsored an event,
and I was asked to play.

–240–

I am writing a book about golf,
so I have to play.

–241–

I'm taking my father out for his birthday.

67

–242–
I have to make sure my back stays loose.

–243–
I just love to golf.

–244–
I lost my keys on the course last year,
and I'm going to keep playing until I find them.

–245–
I have to see how my new lesson worked out.

-246-
I took the day off because
my office is being painted.

-247-
I really just like the scenery on the golf course.

-248-
I want to fix my brother up with the new
woman pro. She's great-looking and can
carry her tee ball 240 yards.

-249-
I'm getting in touch with my inner golfer.

69

–250–

My new socks are supposed to fit in my golf shoes better.

-251-
There is nothing else to do
in northern Wisconsin.

-252-
I lost too many balls playing tennis;
I want to try golf!

-253-
I kept missing the balls playing softball.

-254-
My horse is sick, so polo is
out of the question for today.

-255-
All the cool kids play golf.

-256-
I like watching the geese on the course.

-257-
I have a scramble next week.
I need the practice.

-258-
I gambled away my mortgage money last week,
so I have to win it back.

72

-259-

I am very optimistic I will play well if I golf today, so I'm going!

-260-

My new golf shorts have a special built-in pocket to hold tees.

-261-

It's better than doing the laundry.

-262-

My broker offered to take me.

73

-263-
The clubhouse was just remodeled.

-264-
The greenskeeper just planted
new flowers by the 6th green.

-265-
I just finished taking a lesson on the
Internet; I want to see how I improved.

-266-
It's Augusta!

-267-
I golf every day that ends in a "y."

-268-
It's the only thing to do in Las Vegas.

-269-
My father asked me to teach him...again!

-270-
The doctor ordered me to
get lots of fresh air.

75

-271-

My wife is taking the kids golfing.
I think I'll tag along.

-272-

The mist over the pond by the first tee
reminds me of Scotland.

-273-

My shoulder is finally feeling better.

-274-

I have never played a canyon course before.

–276–
It's easier than doing my taxes.

–277–
It feels great pulling up
ball marks on the green.

–278–
I have some extra money for greens fees
from my company's profit sharing.

–279–
If I wasn't here,
I'd be home cleaning out the basement.

78

-280-

I just like wearing golf shoes;
they are so comfortable.

-281-

I support my family by selling the
golf balls I find in the woods.

-282-

I like going swimming in the
clubhouse pool after I golf.

-283-

Research indicates the more I play,
the better I get.

-284-

My best friend is taking me
golfing for my birthday.

-285-

I've only played 12 rounds this week;
I need Lucky 13.

-286-

I never regret going golfing.

-287-

It's where the taxi took me.

80

-288-
I've never golfed in Scotland before.

-289-
I love the way the sun rises on the fairway.

-290-
I came home from work, and a note instructed me to leave and go golfing.

-291-
I want to try out my new lob wedge.

-292-

I learned a new putting technique,
which makes me only one-putt.

-293-

I need to try my newly regripped clubs.

-294-

That's where they told me to
go for the job interview.

-295-

I was physically forced to join
the company golf league.

-296-

I have to golf; it's a guy thing.

-297-

It's an opportunity to play a course
I have never played before.

-298-

You get a free lunch with
every round of golf.

-299-

I had a dream last night
telling me to go golfing.

-300-

I always play well when the wind blows out of the north.

–301–

I have spent a lot of time practicing;
I want to see how I do.

–302–

I have a coupon from the newspaper.

–303–

It's a habit.

–304–

They put in a new sand trap
on the long par–5 fairway.

85

-305-

They clean my clubs after the round is over.

-306-

Standing over a birdie putt is just thrilling.

-307-

I had to make a sales call
at the course anyway.

-308-

It is an opportunity to meet new friends.

-309-
I need to try my new carry bag.

-310-
My sister asked me to take her.

-311-
They gave me free greens fees
because it was so slow last week.

-312-
I can finally keep my driver in the fairway.

-313-

I want to see if my new ball retriever works.

-314-

I heard the course is flat—
I always play well on flat courses.

-315-

It's the only sport I can take up at my age.

-316-

I need to work on my slice.

88

-317-
I sponsored a hole at the charity event.

-318-
It's the first day of the summer.

-319-
Hunting season is over, so I'm going golfing.

-320-
It was my mom's suggestion.

89

-321-
I have an opportunity to play
with the three best players at the club.

-322-
I had new soft-spikes put on my golf shoes.

-323-
I always play well when it rains.

-324-
I won greens fees in the employee raffle.

90

–325–

I have to see if my new sunglasses really help me read the greens better.

91

-326-

I couldn't find any videos I wanted to watch.

-327-

I just got tungsten irons in the mail.

-328-

I don't have a logo ball from that course.

-329-

I have only played that course on my computer.

92

I just love that moment when the ball goes soaring off into the sky.

I think I can finally beat my wife.

My cell phone is out of range at that course, so my boss can't reach me.

My mom is taking the kids to the amusement park—so I'm taking the afternoon off.

-334-

My house is being remodeled—
I was just in the way.

-335-

It's too hot to work in the yard.

-336-

The fairways are like greens, and
the greens are like velvet.
I just have to play it.

-337-

I really like a good challenge and golf is
the only sport that humbles my ego.

94

-338-

If you buy a dozen golf balls at the pro shop on Tuesdays, they will let you stay and play for free.

-339-

It's a holiday; what else should I do?

-340-

When you pay for 18 holes, you get the second 18 for free.

-341-

The clouds are all white and puffy. Perfect golf clouds.

-342-

The wind is blowing out of the south; I may be able to par the #1 handicap hole.

-343-

It's rained a lot lately.
My long irons will stick the green.

-344-

I lost my work ID,
so I might as well go golfing.

-345-

I quit smoking, and a golf course provides a lot of fresh air.

96

-346-

I gave up intimacy with my wife,
so this is my new vice.

-347-

My football game was snowed out,
but I couldn't just stay home.

-348-

I had a sunroof put in on my golf cart.
I need to try it out.

-349-

They are fumigating my office, so I have to
find something to do this afternoon.

97

–350–
I was laid off, so
I might as well go golfing.

98

-351-

My wife made me join her golf league
so we can spend quality time together.

-352-

The Cubs have a night game,
so I need to golf this afternoon.

-353-

The creek is dried up, so I won't
lose a ball on my approach shot.

-354-

They are having an open house on my home,
so I have to find something to do.

99

-355-

I just can get more business
done on the course.

-356-

They are giving away free golf tees
with every 9 holes purchased.

-357-

I like the feeling of the wind blowing in
my hair when I drive the golf cart.

-358-

All the executives from my
company play this course.

100

-359-

My mom is making me teach
my little brother to golf.

-360-

I had to join the course so my
wife could make some friends.

-361-

A free round of golf was
included with the lessons.

-362-

I may be able to play by myself.
I always score better!

-363-
My next door neighbor asked
if I wanted to go.

-364-
It's the only challenge
I find besides talking with my wife.

-365-
There is a traffic jam, so I might as well
play nine instead of sitting in traffic.

-366-
All the TV shows are reruns.

102

-367-

The voices in my head told me to go golfing.

-368-

I enjoy the smell of freshly cut grass.

-369-

I just returned from Antarctica.
I really am craving the frustration
of playing bad golf.

-370-

The course just installed
new electric golf ball washers.

103

-371-

This course has the best
Philly cheese steaks in town;
I might as well stay and play.

-372-

My wife has custody of the kids for the
next two weeks, so I have plenty of free time.

-373-

This new course has valet parking.

-374-

I like playing cards in the locker room
when I'm done golfing.

104

–376–

I have a new towel that's supposed to
clean my clubs with one swipe.

–377–

We lost electricity in our house.

–378–

The sky is the perfect shade of blue.

–379–

I got new license plates for
my golf cart today.
I want to see how they look.

-380-

I lost my driver's license and the closest place to walk is the golf course.

-381-

My girlfriend bought me a perspiration-free golf shirt.

-382-

On the course is the only place I feel free.

-383-

Church was canceled because of all the snow, so I'm going golfing.

-384-
I just love to golf new courses.

-385-
This course has the best sand traps.

-386-
When I visit my brother,
that's all he does—so I have to golf.

-387-
I've been getting anger management
counseling for my temper on the golf
course—I need to see if it's working.

108

-388-

My grandma cooks such good meals;
the course is the best place to walk it off.

-389-

I like the challenge of the
undulating greens on this course.

-390-

I finally can make my ball go left to right.

-391-

The bachelor party starts on the course.

-392-

I almost broke 90 on my last time out.
I need to keep trying.

-393-

I've never had the chance to
play on bent grass greens before.

-394-

The course put in a new
irrigation system on the back nine.

-395-

The yardage has all been remarked.

-396-
I love long par-3s over ponds.

-397-
The golf course is the only place
I can get my entire family together.

-398-
The humidity is low, so I won't sweat.

-399-
Monday Night Football
moved back to 9:00 P.M.,
so I have the entire evening.

-400-

I have never birdied a #1 handicap hole.

-401-
I just bought a pair of waterproof shoes with the slip-proof soft-spikes.

-402-
The course is trying out a new program with water coolers on all the carts.

-403-
I just had graphite shafts put on my clubs.

-404-
I like to think about life while I golf.

113

–405–

They installed rain guards on the
back of the carts to keep your clubs dry.

–406–

I just bought a box of titanium golf balls.

–407–

Golf fills the long void of the
weekend until work starts again.

–408–

My wife looks sexy carrying golf clubs.

114

-409-
The golf course is the only place
I can take my girlfriend where
she doesn't talk constantly.

-410-
I started to follow through on my swing.

-411-
I just bought a new golf glove off the Web.

-412-
Those new thin tees allow me to
hit my drive an extra ten yards.

-413-
I received a demo package of
the liquid core golf balls.

-414-
I learn from observing the
other player's swing.

-415-
I finally have a chance to play
with someone worse than I am.

-416-
I enjoy looking through the
used golf balls in the pro shop.

-417-

A hot dog just tastes
better on the golf course.

-418-

The course has great golf magazines
in the bathroom stalls.

-419-

Since getting my new camera,
I collect photos of every green.

-420-

The course we are scheduled
to play has a lot of hills.

117

-421-

I just turned 65; now I can play the gold tees.

-422-

I love the decision-making part of golfing.

-423-

I heard they got rid of the
Porta-potty at the turn.
I have to christen the new bathroom.

-424-

I just bought a putter that is guaranteed
to cut ten strokes off my round.

-426-

My carpet at home just doesn't
break like a real green.

-427-

I can finally play under pressure,
so I can start betting again.

-428-

I like playing with these guys;
they don't make me putt out.

-429-

I just got a new yardage gauge.

120

-430-

The new rakes for traps are supposed to allow the ball to fly out of the sand easier.

-431-

Golf brings out my most competitive nature.

-432-

Drinking beer and golfing is just fun.

-433-

You can get the best cigars on the golf course.

-434-
I have been on a plane all day;
I really need some fresh air.

-435-
We might play a links course;
I wouldn't have to see any other golfers.

-436-
My new golf bag has a cooler that
guarantees beer will stay cold for five hours.

-437-
My new shoelaces are guaranteed
to lower my score.

-438-
I like collecting yardage books.

-439-
My wife lets me golf if I go to church.

-440-
I need to try and fish my
driver out of the pond.
I left it there last time I played.

-441-
I like seeing my footprints on
the dew in the early morning.

-442-

I just enjoy having a cup of hot coffee
while waiting on the tee box each morning.

-443-

They just replaced the rye
with bluegrass in the fairways.

-444-

I always play golf on my birthday.

-445-

I just bought some slice-proof tees.

-446-
I played so badly last week;
I just want to get back out.

-447-
My wife only lets me play miniature
golf; I need the real thing.

-448-
I want to play in Denver;
the ball flies farther.

-449-
I like using the ball washers—it's fun.

–450–

Frustration is a rush.
I can only get that
on a golf course.

-451-
I get depressed when I don't play.

-452-
I think I can finally control the ball.

-453-
When the course is dried out,
I can hit the ball a lot farther.

-454-
I'm getting married this afternoon.
I need to sneak in 36.

-455-

I just want to play an
entire round without a shank.

-456-

I dreamed I would shoot even par
if I went out today.

-457-

I usually play strong on the 19th hole.

-458-

I slowed down my backswing. Now
I need to see if it helps my game.

128

–459–

Playing golf helps me get
back my concentration.

–460–

I just won the slice-free driver.

–461–

This course offers free caddies
with each round purchased.

–462–

I like saving score cards
from every round I play.

-463-

The course guarantees no flies or mosquitoes.

-464-

My wife is pregnant, and she
just wants me out of the house.

-465-

They just got all new range balls.

-466-

After reading the USGA rules,
I have to change my theory on golf.

-467-

I just bought winter golf gloves.
I want to see how they work.

-468-

Free beer at the turn.

-469-

The superintendent just replaced
all the sand in the traps.

-470-

I just got the high spin,
titanium-tungsten-liquid-filled golf balls.

131

-471-

I have to take advantage of
free guest day at the club.

-472-

The rain has blown through,
and the sun is shining.

-473-

I missed my flight because security was
backed up, so I might as well go golfing.

-474-

My psychiatrist hypnotized me, and
I am guaranteed to shoot par.

132

-476-
It's the only place I know where women won't bother me.

-477-
My chiropractor has cracked my back, allowing me to extend my follow-through.

-478-
With the wind blowing, I can drive the greens on the par-4s.

-479-
My wife bought me a pair of those golf undergarments.

134

-480-
They are offering a free round of golf with a night's stay at this hotel; I'm considering moving in permanently.

-481-
I enjoy wearing golf caps.

-482-
I am useless at work unless I golf twice a week.

-483-
I want to find out if the Zen Oracle Putting Trainer has actually helped me.

-484-

My wife went shopping and asked me
not to be home when she returns.

-485-

The softball game was rained out.

-486-

I want to try the new glow-in-the-dark
golf balls I bought yesterday.

-487-

The course is going to
aerate the greens next week.

-488-

A free round of golf was
thrown in for test driving the car.

-489-

The wind is blowing.

-490-

I was late for my job interview,
so I might as well go golfing.

-491-

My wife is busy washing the dog.
I think I can sneak out the back door.

137

-492-

My team didn't make the playoffs;
now I'm off in the afternoons.

-493-

My wife went house hunting with her sister.

-494-

My grandma instructed me to go.

-495-

I'm hopelessly addicted to golfing.

-496-

I like seeing the fish in the
ponds when I look for my ball.

138

–497–

I just rarely get the opportunity
to play that course.

–498–

It is the perfect place to
teach my son anger control.

–499–

The speed of play on this course is excellent.

–500–

I like reading long putts.

–501–

Excuse? I don't need no stinkin' excuse.

139

About the Author

Justin J. Exner is an airline executive with a BA in Aviation Business from Embry-Riddle Aeronautical University in Daytona Beach, Florida, and an MBA from Franklin University in Columbus, Ohio. He has played golf all over the world, never without a good reason. Justin golfs regularly and three-putts very frequently. He lives with his family in Haymarket, Virginia.